A Multi-unicultural Inclusion Mexican Regional Dances For Performing Arts

Dr. Paul A. Rodríguez

Cogito Consulting, LLC

Dr. Paul A. Rodríguez

ISBN-10: 0-9863065-4-1
ISBN-13: 978-0-9863065-4-9

DEDICATION

I dedicate this project to my children Harmonie Mae, Alexander Faustino, and Paul Anthony Rodriguez, II. May this project encourage them to appreciate and strive for a knowledgeable interest in philosophy, education, and music.

Finally, posthumously for my parents, Maria Fernández Rodriguez (R.I.P. 1991) and Salvador Zuñiga Rodriguez (R.I.P. 1992).

CONTENTS

PART II

Dr. Paul A. Rodríguez

ACKNOWLEDGMENTS

I thank Dr. Constance Lim and Dr. Cecilia Cota-Robles de Suárez for their unceasing encouragement and understanding throughout this endeavor. Also, Manuel A. Castillejos for his insight on Mexican folklore and culture. I especially thank my wife, Doreen, for her patience and in understanding my continuing commitment to education, philosophy, and music.

PART 1

CHAPTER 1

INTRODUCTION

Dance, the most ancient of arts, has been an integral part of religious customs and rituals. It is important to the socialization process in civilization. Dance can made a significant contribution to the curriculum with human development and expression. The Visual and Performing Arts

Framework (California State Board of Education, 1989) asserted that:

> The dance experience is an ideal instrument for developing and enriching bilingual and Multicultural programs because dance is a nonverbal medium. (p. 30)

Participation in dances of other cultures enables the student to experience feelings, sensations, and ideas associated with those cultures. Students can sense the rich contributions of the multiethnic and Multicultural groups, past and present, that makes the American society. Saxe (1989) stated:

> I have pointed out that democracy in our nation serves a pluralistic society, but that this society needs a cultural currency to function efficiently. Harmon is found in diversity, not sameness. Likewise, democracy is a result of collective sharing among willing participants seeking substance and unity. (pp. 199-200)

The very complexity and diversity within our American society coheres for the inclusion of multiculturalism in dance education curriculum. Many dances draw upon dances of other cultures. An appreciation of the similarities and distinctions of various cultures is gained through the study of folk dance. Dance reflects the personality and temperament of a people that gives dance its lasting appeal.

Likewise, researchers inform us that the brain operates on an emotional bias system. Information that is perceived by the learner as helpful, interesting, rewarding (Hart,

1975; Sagan, 1977), and or gamey is eventually processed by the brain. In short, we learn what we want to learn. Cognitive functioning is determined by the emotional state of the learner (Galyean, 1981). Many dance movements can signify universal shared meanings. Viewed as a universal language, symbolized through dance, furthers the child's knowledge of the world and its diverse cultures. Exposure to dance helps children understand and appreciate their own culture and the cultures of others.

Subsequently, dance constitutes a mean for helping students learn how to live in peace, harmony, and mutual respect in a complex, pluralistic society.

The information presented in this book enriches and develops in students the knowledge and appreciation of our multicultural dance heritage. Likewise, students come to recognize dance as a universal language in world cultures. Dance is a nonverbal communicative skill which processes mainly from the appositional hemisphere of the brain. Logan (1984) concluded that "Dance experiences allow the child to view the aesthetic dimension of movement and heighten kinesthetic awareness and bodily intelligence" (p. 300). Likewise, Hawkins (1964) affirmed: "Dance as a work of art may be described as the expression of man's inner feelings transformed by imagination and given form through the medium of movement"

(p. 4). Few efforts in educational systems have designed a comprehensive developmental sequence of dance education for all students before the university or college level. Schwartz (1991) stated that:

> Multicultural dance provides a means of understanding cultural differences and helps students understand and clarify their own value systems. Educators communicate values to students through their educational structures that, in dance, cross barriers of language, culture, and nationality. (p. 46)

There needs to be an opportunity for the average teacher to have a variety of materials, other than a textbook, to create and develop in their students an appreciation for multicultural dance. Thus, this book was developed as handbook on selected Mexican regional dances for use in the K-6 grade classrooms. Dance as a creative experience offers an alternative mode of expression. The student will be able to recognize dance as a nonverbal universal language in world cultures—past, present, and future.

The literature researched revealed that the elementary curriculum needs to incorporate multicultural dance into its curriculum. Dance, as an art form, has been an integral part of many cultural heritages. It is important to the socialization process in civilization. Our American society is very diverse and complex. Schwartz (1991) stated that within the United States all its people have roots in other lands, and that we are indeed a nation of immigrants.

The study of dance can make a significant contribution to the development of human expression. Participating in dances of other cultures enables the student to experience feelings, sensations, and ideas associated with those cultures (Rosengren, Wiley, & Wiley, 1983). Students can sense the contributions of the multiethnic and multicultural groups that make the American society. Ramirez (1989) indicated that dance exemplifies the heart of the people and this art form needs to be cultivated to give people a sense of pride and identity.

Furthermore, during the concrete operational state (ages 7-11) children become increasingly competent of mental actions that are reversible relying on concrete objects that are physically present. Henceforth, children need a learning environment that provides for hands-on activities and interesting objects that promote real-life experiences. Combining the arts into the curriculum provides opportunities to unify mental representations symbolically for the child.

Gardner (1983) expanded on a new theory of intelligence. Gardner recognized seven areas of intelligence. They are: linguistic, musical, logical-mathematical, spatial, bodily-kinesthetic, interpersonal, and intrapersonal. Our educational system has in the past focused mainly on two intelligences, those being linguistic and logical-mathematical. Gardner redefined an intelligence as those activities which create products which are greatly valued within one or more cultural backgrounds. In embracing this redefinition of intelligence, our views about the arts and their function in school curriculum and environments change. The arts encourages the child to participate and interact where every child can contribute and discover.

As educators, we need to be knowledgeable to multicultural

education and at the same time be sensitive to the educational needs of ethnic minority children (Social Education, 1989). The California Visual and Performing Arts Framework (California State Board of Education, 1989) acknowledged the importance of incorporating a multicultural perspective throughout the visual and performing arts curriculum. Rosengren et al. (1983) contended that multicultural educational is capable of measuring diversity as a force for human emancipation and facilitating dignity among diverse groups.

Lastly, as our nation moves toward the recognition of a multiethnic cultural diversity, it becomes extremely pertinent to advocate a multicultural educational environment. The uniqueness and strength of our nation is found in the diversity of its people (Saxe, 1989). While increasing our knowledge and cultivation of our multicultural heritage, we strengthen our future. Through the nonverbal universal language of dance, we as a people can learn mutual respect and harmony in our complex, pluralistic society.

One major purpose of education is to develop capacities that are inherently common to all children. Students will view the arts as a means of acquiring cultural literacy. Likewise, students will study aesthetics and cultural heritage which are the continuing impact of the arts on all societies worldwide. Viewing the arts at a deeper and significant level helps the student see works of art as bodies of knowledge which define every culture. In so doing, students become aware that the arts cut across cultural boundaries to provide mutual appreciation, understanding, and respect.

In addition, the students' emotional capacities and needs can be developed and fulfilled through music. Musical-experience activities help build self-esteem, imaginative responses, motivational, and positive attitudes in the students. The experiences develop a positive sense of involvement and concentration of attention in movement exploration, expression, and communication. Gardner (1990) believed that children make sense of their world when educational experiences are focused on their individual styles of learning and discovery. Combining the arts into every educational curriculum cultivates the uniqueness and multiculturalism of every child.

Likewise, some aspects of music will enhance the students'

intellectual and aesthetic capacities. These aspects will cultivate the intellectual bases for making and justifying aesthetic judgments in dance about personal and values, and to the environment. The student will relate the basic elements of dance to aesthetic qualities and other areas of study (California State Board of Education, 1990).

Finally, through dance the student will identify the place of dance as a means of communication throughout human history. The student will associate and compare dance styles from historical and cultural perspectives. These universal themes and values are exemplified in the selected Mexican regional dances of this project.

For this book, it is assumed that our educational system has a responsibility to expand the positive self-esteem of all students. Likewise, public educational institutions have the responsibility to provide all students with an opportunity to experience the cultures of their peers. In developing an awareness and an aesthetic appreciation of other cultures, students will deal more desirably with diverse people in our pluralistic society.

Cultural differences must be acknowledged in students to celebrate their diversity and contributions to society. In educational institutions, students should develop respect for the human dignity of all people and be offered opportunities to express their own creativity by providing direct, hands-on experiences in the various art forms.

Lastly, if the teacher is fervent at the prospect of learning about other cultures, the students will be as well. The teacher will train students how to listen to, look at, and think about art by training their analytical faculties and critical acumen.

The information within this book may be used as a resource to develop lessons not included or that have more meaning to the students with whom the teacher is currently working. As ethnic cultures vary from school to school, some cultures may not be included in the project. It will be the responsibility of those using this guide to modify the lessons presented to meet their needs.

This information within the book will focus only with eight selected secular Mexican regional dances. The dances are: *El Baile de Los Viejitos, El Jarabe Tapatio, El Jarabe de La Botalla, La Zandunga, La Banba, Las Chapanecas, Jarable*

Michoacano, and *Jarana Yucateca*. The dances were selected according to availability and grade-level appropriateness. The book does not speak to factors such as writing, language arts, or mathematics.

Definition of Terms

- Aesthetic is the search and appreciation for beauty.
- Appositional describes the type of cognition proper to the right hemisphere, in contrast to the common use by neurologists or

propositional for the left hemisphere (Bogen, 1973).

- Cooperative Learning is a process that enables the student to listen to others, evaluate the problem, and make decisions for the common good of the group. It develops negotiating skills to work toward solutions that are the goals of the group (Geiger & Rodriguez, 1993).
- Vulture is created by people in social environments and systems composed of unique

beliefs, values, traditions, language, customs, technology, and institutions as a way of meeting basic human needs shaped by their own physical environments and contact with other cultures (Kniep, 1989).

- Ethnic Group is related to a group of people who are bound together by language, religious, or cultural ties (Banks, 1976).

- Ethnic Minority Group is an ethnic group with several distinguishing characteristics. Although an ethnic minority group, like an ethnic group, shares a common culture, a historic tradition, and a sense of peoplehood, it also has unique physical and/or cultural characteristics that enable individuals who belong to other groups to identify its members easily, often for discriminatory purposes. Ethnic minority groups also tend to be a numerical minority and to exercise little political and economic power (Banks, 1984).

- Hands-on Experience is a process that enables the student to listen to others, evaluate the problem, and make decisions for the common good of the group. It develops negotiating skills to work toward solutions that are the goals of the group (Geiger & Rodriguez, 1993).

- Left Brain refers to the left hemisphere of the brain that deals with verbal, analytical, rational, logical, and linear functioning. Bogen (1973) called this mode 'propositional' to avoid only value judgments about which hemisphere is superior.
- Mult-iunicultural is the concept that prior to understanding and

acknowledging other cultures individuals must first comprehend and embrace their own unique beliefs, values, traditions, language, customs, and physical environment (Rodriguez, 1994).

- Nonverbal is the human expression of ideas and feelings without oral speech or written symbols.
- Pluralism is a concept in which different groups

maintain their individuality while functioning effectively in society (Weaver, 1988).

- Propositional categorizes the linear, logical, analytic 'if . . . then' processing of the left hemisphere, in contrast to appositional thought. A mental process highly receptive to codified knowledge (Bogen, 1973).
- Right Brain refers to the right hemisphere of the brain that deals with visual, holistic, non-verbal,

emotions, and movement functioning. Bogen (1973) called this mode 'appositional' to avoid any value judgments about which hemisphere is superior. When both hemispheres work together, the capacity for two minds exists

CHAPTER 2

STUDY OF DANCE

The review of the literature revealed material available for the elementary curriculum concerning multicultural dance. Dance, the most ancient of arts, has been an integral part of religious customs and rituals. It is important to the socialization process in civilization. Our American society is very diverse and complex. Schwartz (1991) argued that "One in four

Americans is a person of color. Almost all of us have roots in other lands, and that we are indeed a nation of immigrants".

The study of dance can make a significant contribution to the curriculum with human development and expression. Participation in dances of other cultures enables the student to experience feelings, sensations. and ideas associated with those cultures. Students can sense the rich contributions of the multiethnic and multicultural groups, past and present which make the American society. Schwartz (1991) acknowledges that:

> American modern dancers and dance educators have long known that dance from various cultures enriches the art with which they are engaged. Multiculturalism is part and parcels of our modern dance heritage. (p. 46)

This book of multicultural dance is important to our American heritage and should be examined thoroughly. Students should not only be taught dance technique, but likewise the cultural and historical contexts of dances. As Posey (1988) indicated:

> The ability to draw upon knowledge from cultural and historical dance and to analyze and interpret dance choreography and performance is as important as the student's ability to move well. (p. 62)

Dance characterizes the "soul of the people;" consequently, "these practices should be actively cultivated to give people a sense of pride and identity" (Ramírez, 1989, p. 18).

HISTORY OF MEXICAN REGIONAL DANCE

México has a tremendous wealth of folk music and dances, many of them are made up of an ancient heritage. Folk music exists everywhere in México. Following the conquest, the Spaniards employed native musicians because they did not have any of their own. But later ignored them because they did not need them. Today folk music and musicians are greatly appreciated more than ever (Toor, 1947)

Prior to the conquest only men and boys played musical instruments, but the boys and girls learned to sing and dance together throughout their lives. Only boys received musical instruction after the Conquest in the first Catholic schools. The most famous being the one established by Fray Pedro de Grante to Texcoco in 1527 (Toor, 1947). Many natives became good musicians and were also skillful in making copies of the European instruments (Dickins, 1954). Within a short period of time, there were a sufficient number of skilled musicians for the numerous churches established. However, this form of musical education and training conflicted with the main interest of the Spanish conquerors. They felt that the natives were becoming too educated and spending too much time in schools. Consequently, the indigenous people were not permitted to attend the schools and educate themselves. Thus, the schools were closed and the work of the missionaries came to an abrupt end.

Nevertheless, the musical education of the people continued, but not on a religious theme. The merchants found that they could sell more liquor by teaching the people to sing and play guitars. With the leniency of the laws and the opportunistic merchants, México was flooded with intoxicating drinks (Toor, 1947).

As time went on women sang less. Except for the Seri and Huichol women and girls, singing was done in church. One would seldom hear a woman singing at her work. The people sang less after the Conquest because only those who are free and happy sing (Toor, 1947).

Since the 1910-1920 Revolution, conditions have changed. The people feel freer and are encouraged to sing. They need no longer fear to raise their voices or to sing their songs. Folk music is now popular everywhere. People sing and dance more than ever before and express the entire gamut of their emotions through their music.

All the dances for secular folk dances are in the form of songs, called *sones, jarabes* and *huapangos*, the latter having a very marked rhythm. Most tunes are light and gay; the verses picaresque and tender.

It would be impossible to describe all the ritual and secular dances. No one has listed all known dances and they are different in every region of México. Their varieties are as numerous as the places in which they are danced. However, all the dances, in general, express the vast emotional gamut of the Mexican people's diversified culture. The dances selected are post Spanish conquest mestizo dances, which combine Spanish and Indian elements.

STATUS OF MULTICULTURAL EDUCATION

The status of multicultural education has become a very important factor in today's educational system. Our educational system must provide an avenue for children to develop into production and contributing citizens. There is a legitimacy for diversity and multicultural education at all levels of the curriculum of instruction (Baptiste, 1979). Hollins (1982) asserted the need for the creating of a multicultural theory of learning. Accordingly, Hollins stated that Piaget's theory did not allow for cultural differences in the onset of the various stages. It was found that most other learning theories also lacked a multicultural or cross-cultural dimension. Therefore, it is important to formulate a multicultural learning theory that would take into account the cultural bias inherent in most related research.

Individuality and culture are interrelated. Multicultural education must view learners as not only contributors to society and the educational system, but also to themselves (Francis, 1992). A multi-unicultural perspective must be integrated into the educational system. A multi-unicultural concept allows individuals to first comprehend and embrace their own unique beliefs, values, traditions, language, customs, and physical environment prior to understanding and acknowledging other cultures. Our American educational system has not always promoted person oneness and identity, but has advocated a Eurocentric orientation of losing the majority of one's own culture through the blending of another. The history of our American educational system has at times ignored the cultural diversity of society (Francis, 1992).

ASPECTS OF MULTICULTURAL EDUCATION

Our school environments should enhance the students' emotional well-being and positive self-esteem. In spite of the fact that prejudices cannot be completely eliminated, much can be done to make the school environment a better one for all students. Cultural-awareness activities can involve school personnel, students, and the community members. These activities can sensitize people to the needs and feelings of others.

The California History Social Science Framework (History-Social Science Framework, 1987) and the Visual and Performing Arts Framework for California Public

Schools (California State Board of Education, 1989), both promote the importance of integrating a multicultural perspective into our instructional curriculum. "Dance students can sense the rich contributions of the multiethnic and multicultural groups, past and present, which make up the American Heritage (California State Board of Education, 1989, p. 30). Likewise, teachers are called to 'acknowledge that the history of community, state, region, nation and world must reflect the experience of all people from different racial, religious and ethnic groups' (History-Social Science Framework, 1987, p. 5).

Multicultural education definition:

1. Cultural diversity is seen as a positive reality in the United States.
2. Cultural diversity is viewed as a valuable resource to be preserved and utilized.
3. Cultural diversity and cultural differences are a

valuable and vital force in the development of our society.

4. Acknowledges the belief in our Constitution for the respect of each individual regardless of ethnicity, race, religion, sex, socioeconomic status, physical or mental ability.
5. Strives to blend affective and cognitive growth.
6. Within the requirement of national unity acknowledges

the integrity of group cultures.

Multicultural Education Goals:

1. To develop a positive self-image in order to understand one's own culture and develop an appreciation for the culture of others.
2. To develop an understanding of one's own value systems, cultures, customs and histories, as well as others outside of oneself.

3. To develop an appreciation of individual and cultural differences.
4. To provide a base for productive participation in one or more cultures.
5. To develop a desire to contribute to and grow in a culturally diverse nation and world.
6. To develop a respect for freedom and dignity of others, and to accept the responsibility for sustaining

> and increasing the institutions of all people in a multicultural and interdependent society, in order to contribute to a greater freedom for all. (Chapman, 1983)

Kniep (1989) noted that instructors should give students a basic knowledge of the values of their own cultures and society. Likewise, students should be encouraged to examine the values of others and see the commonality and diversity among people. Saxe

(1989) concurred that in order to have harmony in our society instructors need to look to the diversity of individuals to realize collective sharing and unity.

> I point out that democracy in our nation serves a pluralistic society, this society needs a cultural currency to function efficiently. Educators at all levels need to seek the common ground, to examine the roots and history of the foundational studies as well as the social studies in order to harmonize their positions in the curriculum. (p. 400)

CHAPTER 3

THEORETICAL FOUNDATIONS OF THE ARTS

There are several theoretical groundworks for the developmental learning of children. Careful investigation of the various developmental theories can lead to genuine ways of traversing behaviors and situations. The examination of these forms of theories can manifest an opportunity for cogitation and comprehension of experiences. Therefore, educational practice becomes a circumstance that enhances learning for both students and instructor.

INTELLECTUAL DEVELOPMENT

Through the clinical researcher, Jean Piaget, we have learned that children think differently and progress through a qualitative path to maturity. Children of school-age make the transition from the preoperational stage of development (ages 2-6) to the concrete operational state (ages 7-11).

Within the preoperational stage children are capable to think of and imagine objects and events not physically present. While in the concrete operational period, children become increasing competent of mental actions that are reversible relying on concrete objects that are physically present. Consequently, reinforcing the mental growth of children adheres to learning environments that provide for hands-on activities and interesting objects that promote real life experiences. The experiences and activities become the basis for the children's stored mental images and mental representations. Integrating the arts, such as, drama, music, art, storytelling, poems, movement, and dance into the curriculum provides opportunities to integrate mental representations symbolically for the child. The student's intellectual development is increased in a motivating, interesting. and fun way.

According to Piaget (1985) children learn new knowledge

through active discovery based on their experiences and their immediate levels of cognitive development. Henceforth, children need to participate in activities that provide opportunities for expressive play, exploration. and discovery. Adler (1968) stated:

> Of all the organs with which a child attempts the conquest of the world, the sense organs are the most important in the determination of the essential relationships to the world in which he lives. It is through the sense organs that

> one constructs one's cosmic picture. (p. 45)

Gardner developed a new theory of intelligence. Gardner identified seven intelligences:

1. Linguistic: the ability to use language to excite, please, convince, stimulate, or convey information.

2. Musical: the ability to enjoy, perform, or compose a musical piece.

3. Logical – mathematical: the ability to explore patterns, categories, and relationships by manipulating objects or

symbols, and to experience in a controlled, orderly way.

4. Spatial: the ability to perceive and mentally manipulate a form or object, to perceive and create tension, balance, and composition in a visual or spatial display.

5. Bodily-kinesthetic: the ability to use fine and gross motor skills in sports, the performing arts, or arts and craft production.

6. Interpersonal: the ability to understand and get along with others.

7. Intrapersonal: the ability to gain access to and understand one's inner feelings, dreams and ideas. (Hatch & Gardner, 1988, p. 38)

Our educational system has in the past focused on two intelligences, those being linguistic and logical-mathematical. Gardner (1983) defined an intelligence as those activities which create products or the ability to solve problems which are greatly valued within one or more cultural backgrounds. Accepting this redefinition of intelligence expands our view of the arts and its function in school curriculum and environments.

SOCIAL DEVELOPMENT

Vygotsky (1978) asserted that higher mental functions are formed through social interaction and result in the transmission of culture. Interaction with other individuals helps the child understand his own feelings and the feelings of others. In so doing, through the interpersonal interaction and contact with various objects and individuals, the child will achieve fundamental pre-requisites for aesthetic practice. As Gardner (1973) asserted:

> Development of the self through imitation and communication is an unconscious as well as a conscious process, and, a person's sense of self, his identity, to use the current parlance, is an enormously complex and subtle phenomenon. (p. 95)

Therefore, if social interactions are important, "then the classroom environment must stimulate discussions about literature, favorite paintings and photographs, and most-loved music" (Cecil & Lauritzen, 1994, p. 5). The arts encourage participation and interaction where every child can contribute and discover. As Gardner (1973) enunciated:

> Indeed, if the arts involve communication of information about subjective experience, the initial manifestation of such communication may be crucial; 'truth' or 'genuineness' in works of art may reflect the sense of

> well-being and veridicality also paramount in encounters with human beings. (p. 97)

Teachers and parents can help children develop their artistic creativity and understanding with exposure to artist and their works. In so doing, art might become more real and less remote. Gardner (1982) stated that if children in the early grades could follow a creation of a painting from beginning to end, they might better understand the difference between an object and its representation.

> Indeed, if children are left to acquire understanding on their own, the whole domain of the arts may remain for them as distant as a star, as mysterious as the speaker of a dead language. (Gardner, 1982, p. 109)

EMOTIONAL DEVELOPMENT

Gardner (1990) suggested that there are at least five different kinds of knowledge that any individual who grows up in a schooled environment must ultimately attempt to master and integrate.

Children during their first years of life obtain a large amount of knowledge by virtue of their interactions with physical objects and with other persons. Much of this knowledge is acquired through sensory perceptions and motor interactions, and is developed through the stimulations of these faculties. There is an understanding "about the predictable behavior of objects in the environment, the motivations and intentions of other persons, the physical appearance of familiar entities, and other universally accessible forms of information" (Gardner, 1990, p. 26).

Within the second stage of knowledge, individuals begin to use and to master the most widely available symbol systems of their culture, for example words, pictures, gestures, musical patterns, and the like. The materialization of these cognitive inclinations is facilitated by rich and varied exposure (Cecil & Lauritzen, 1994, p. 6).

Around the age of five to seven, children begin to display signs that they wish to employ various kinds of notational systems, which are usually termed 'notational systems' (Vygotsky, 1978). These notational systems have evolved in literate cultures in order to refer especially to the first-order symbol systems. Gardner (1990) explained that:

> written language refers to oral language; written numerical systems, both oral and sensorily known

> quantitative information; written musical notational systems [that] capture the defining features of music valued in the culture; . . . other important symbolic an intuitive lessons. (p. 26)

Many individuals will proceed to develop their own forms of notation, but it is probable that such systems would not develop without the prior existence of model cultural notations.

The fourth form of knowledge is the mastery of various concepts, principles, and formal bodies of knowledge that researchers, scholars, and reflective human beings have discovered, invented and/or codified over the centuries. Gardner (1990) believed that without formal schooling, there is very little probability that the average person in society would be exposed to them and virtually no chance that they would master them.

Lastly, the fifth form of knowledge, Gardner identified as 'skilled knowledge.' All cultures shelter a collection of crafts, disciplines, and practices that need mastery by some individuals, in order for the knowledge of that society to be passed on to the next generation.

In conclusion, human development must embrace all the various aspects of experiences which uniquely constitute the whole person. Educational systems often maintain that the arts are solely opportunities for self-expression, rather than, means of reaching intellectual development. The integration of the arts into every educational curriculum fosters the uniqueness and multi-uniculturalism of each child. Children make sense of their world when educational experiences are focused on their individual styles of learning and discovery.

CHAPTER 4

EDUCATIONAL VALUE OF DANCE

Dance has been a way of expression and sensitivity throughout human existence. Children are natural movers and spontaneous movement-play. Logan (1984) believed that "What more fitting way for children to harness their energy and imagination than to give form to that movement expression—to dance?" (p. 37). All children should be given the opportunity to participate in dance regardless of their gender. As Stinson (1989) proclaimed, "Even more important, these exploratory experiences contribute to the life of every child, not just those little girls who dream of wearing a tutu" (p. 205).

Traditionally, dance as an art form is one of the least understood. Sparshott (1990) asserted that "Dance is in a curious situation in the public consciousness of the arts" (p. 77). Heretofore, "Dance is an art form that is characterized by use of the human body as a vehicle of expression" (Overby, 1992, p. 1). No special equipment is needed, just the ability to move. Until recently, dance was taught mainly as an activity in the physical education curriculum. It is now recognized as an "art form comparable to music, drama, and visual arts, equally worthy of study" (Carter, 1984, p. 295). Children demystify the aesthetic dimensions of dance movement through sound and movement. When children know what is involved in making and performing dance, it enables them to look at it with sharpened perception and insight.

Although dance is an eloquent art form, it is, however, a non-verbal one that does not lend itself to the normal modes of cognitive investigation. For these reason, students do not gain ready access to dance, especially in educational systems that value more linear approaches to learning.

Logan (1984) maintained that:

> Like the other arts, dance gives us access to a nonverbal metaphoric dimension of experience, one that has to be experienced to be understood; and yet, once children go beyond the early elementary grades, this mode of learning is neglected and ignored. (p. 38)

Lastly, when dance movement activities and sensations of moving are associated to the expressive and imaginative elements of the mover, dance commences. With dance appreciation. the child heightens his kinesthetic awareness, bodily intelligence. and sharpens his perception of movement as a dimension of aesthetic experience.

MULTICULURAL PERSPECTIVES OF DANCE

Dance has become a foremost force of expression among minorities in the United States. Trujillo (1979) stated that "It serves the purpose of ethnic unity, identity, and cultural expression" (p. 1). Yet, Americans know very little about dance. The culturally literate

American knows absolutely nothing about dancing or the dance except that this is something called ballet. Sparshott (1990) enunciated that "He knows about that because his granddaughter wants to grow up to be a ballerina. And, oh yes—didn't there use to be that couple who were in movies back in the thirties?" (p. 74).

The United States is not an effective cultural community. The most important goal in any cultural community is to provide a core of assumptions about the range of what a person is expected to know. Within that community there should be an educational system that supplies every citizen with the means of mastering that range. Olneck (1990) stated that:

> People of color have argued that what is important to their concerns and self-esteem has been relatively unimportant to the dominant society who believes that they alone should decide whose knowledge is to be counted and whose is to be disqualified. (p. 35)

Yet the concept of ethnic diversity is not new or specific. Multicultural education has become an increasingly important factor in the education of our nation's children. Possibly educators are realizing that it is important to develop multicultural curricula and teaching strategies, and that the history of America's multicultural inheritance is unfinished. Marich (1991) protested that people of color have angrily pointed their finger at "Eucocentric curricular offerings and the dominant 'left-brain' way of knowing the world" (p. 4). We must formulate new multicultural models for dance education and recognize its value in multicultural education. In so doing, students will explore their peers' complex cultural dimensions.

Multicultural education must perceive the learner as contributors to society, the educational system and to themselves. It can focus on individuality and enhance the child's freedom to enrich and design their lives. Multicultural education is capable of measuring diversity as a force for human emancipation and facilitating dignity among groups (Rosengren et al., 1983).

MULTICULTURAL ASPECTS OF DANCE CURRICULUM

Studies show that the number of ethnic minority children is increasing. Teachers need to be versed in multicultural education to teach about it, and at the same time to be sensitive to the educational needs of minority children (Social Education, 1989). The California

Visual and Performing Arts Framework (California State Board of Education, 1989) recognized the importance of incorporating a multicultural perspective throughout the visual and performing arts curriculum. The Visual and Performing Arts Frameworks recognized that:

> The teacher is able to illustrate how basic American dance education relates to all cultural forms of dance. In fact, students, through their own dance work, can make creative

> contributions to their changing culture. (p. 31)

Within a multicultural education framework, cultural diversity is seen as a positive reality in the United States and a valuable resource that must be served and utilized. Likewise, cultural diversity and cultural differences are a valuable vital force in the development of our society. Our historical heritage acknowledges that belief in our Constitution for respect of each individual regardless of ethnicity, race, religion, sex, socioeconomic status, physical or mental ability, and strives to blend affective and cognitive growth. Lastly, within the requirements of national unity, educators acknowledge the integrity of group cultures (Francis, 1992).

The goal of the multicultural education curriculum has been based on a developed positive self-esteem, an appreciation for one's culture, and the culture of others. Also, it develops an appreciation of individual and cultural differences, and provides a base for productive participation in one or more cultures. Likewise, it develops a desire to contribute to grow in a culturally diverse nation and world. Lastly, it develops a respect for freedom and dignity of others, and to accept the responsibility for sustaining and increasing the institutions of all people in a multicultural and interdependent society, to contribute to a greater freedom for all. Similarly, it offers a large spectrum of choices in careers, choices involving culturally evolved lifestyles and which are based on each individual's desires, aspirations, and capabilities.

Schwartz (1991) argued that the complexity and diversity within our American society adhere for the inclusion of multiculturalism in dance education curriculum.

> Much of modern dance draws upon dances of other cultures, and through a study of folk dance, an appreciation of the similarities and distinctions of various cultures is also gained. Dance may be used as one of many windows to

> the history, religions and customs of people. (p. 46)

In conclusion, the status of dance education is that at least 15 states have developed dance curriculum guidelines, including California. However, except for North Carolina, no states have mandated that the guidelines be implemented (Gingrasso and Stinson, 1989). Likewise, as Howe (1989) affirmed, "Teachers must be introduced to and receive training in dance so that they can include it appropriately within their lesson plans" (p. 46).

Many of the curriculum guides contain specific content, goals, objectives, and limited measurable outcomes for such areas as:

1. Dance techniques for social, modern, and ethnic dance
2. Aesthetic perception
3. Kinesthetic sense
4. Creative expression
5. Choreography
6. Dance criticism

While many cultures have embraced dance as an integral part of religious customs and rituals, accordingly, Cecil & Lauritzen (1994) asserted that dance serves no significance in American culture. Children are exposed to the role of audience or at the most part an amateur performance or two (p. 109). Dance movements can signify universal shared meanings. Symbolizing through dance, as in language, furthers the child's knowledge of the world and its diverse cultures. Likewise, dance's interwoven exchange between motor and cognitive activities makes it a unique way of accepting and formulating knowledge.

In considering a wholesome dance curriculum educators should consider the following:

1. Exposure to dance helps children understand and appreciate their own culture and the cultures of others.

2. The basic components of dance are pivotal concepts in many other curricular areas and can

therefore be integrated with and enhance mathematics, social sciences, and language arts.

3. Dance provides an intuitive, affective mode of knowing through kinesthetic expression.

4. Lastly, dance as an avenue of self-expression affords an alternative way of being successful for ESL learners and other children who do not or cannot respond successfully to verbal instruction. (Cecil & Lauritzen, 1994, p. 109)

Finally, children will be able to demonstrate through movement that dance is a form of communication and that the variety of movement comes from the uniqueness of each individual's expression. The student should develop a knowledge and appreciation of our multi-unicultural dance heritage and recognize the dance as a universal language in world cultures.

As our nation moves from a majority of Anglo-Americans to one of multiethnic cultural diversity, it becomes increasingly important to promote a multi-unicultural education program. What makes our nation strong and unique is our diversity of people. Increasing the awareness of our multicultural dance heritage strengthens our future in an ever changing cosmos. Likewise, culture not only involves the physical environment, but also what happens in the environment and how people feel about what happens there. Flinchbaugh (1993) stated that culture not only embraces the thoughts and feelings of individuals but leads them to act in certain ways. Cultural identity 'involves the inter-relationships people have with each other' and 'cognitive substance because much of what people do evolves from their thoughts' (p. 49). Students should be taught in ways that enable them to develop knowledge, skills, and good attitudes. Also, there should be a social environment, climate, or culture that supports learning. Similarly, there needs to be a sense of community where mutual sharing among professionals and students is strengthened and active individual and group cooperation and collaboration by both professionals and students is encouraged. The integration of dance education and all the arts provide a unique and needed diversity within the school setting by involving the child's physical as well as the mental processes. Thereby, this inclusion often reaches children who do not respond easily to verbal approaches alone. The dance experience enhances the student's self-esteem, personal identification, and self-motivation. Through the art form of dance, individuals can learn how to truly live in peace, harmony, and mutual respect in our complex, diverse society.

SUMMARY

Within a multicultural educational framework, cultural diversity is seen as a positive reality in the United States and requires a global approach for instruction. All peoples, nations, and culture contribute and grow in a culturally diverse nation and world. It is within our historical heritage to acknowledge and respect each individual regardless of ethnicity, race, religion, sex, socioeconomic status, physical, or mental ability. We must recognize and embrace the integrity of all group cultures.

Lastly, students need to develop their uniqueness and individual expression. An increasing awareness and appreciation of our multi-unicultural dance heritage strengthens our future as a nation. Our dance heritage must be recognized as a universal language in world cultures and as an experience which enhances the student's self-esteem, personal identification, and self motivation.

RECOMMENDATIONS

Indubitably, educators as well as our political representatives must become more actively involved in promoting a multicultural educational environment for all people. Lack of involvement promotes shallow promises, broken spirits, and forgotten dreams. Promises for promoting a multicultural educational framework become worthless words written on paper. They must remember that our American society adheres for the inclusion of multiculturalism on all level of the educational system. Educators and our political representatives must embrace diversity not shun its importance and richness. Acceptance begins with the uniqueness and complexity that each individual has to offer our American society. The United States is neither a monocultural nor monolingual society, which is not exclusively attributed with the dominant societies' belief, but a nation measureable with the diversity of its people and complexity of their cultural heritage. The diversity of the American society is as vast as the stars in the heavens. Likewise, many within the dominant societies' mentality would inclusively bury their heads in the sands of their own benevolence, rather than gaze into the buried mirror of their own uniqueness and diversity. Unfortunately, ignorance and socialistic-psychological fears contribute more for this behavior and frame of thought. Furthermore, the integration of multi-unicultural dance and all the arts provide a uniqueness, enrichment and needed diversity within our school setting, and national psychology which embraces the physical as well as the mental processes of each child. Surely, through the culturally embracing art form of dance, individuals of many cultural heritages will learn how to truly live in peace, harmony, and mutual respect in our ever changing, complex, diversified society.

REFERENCES

Adler, A. (1968). *Understanding human nature.* London: George Allen & Unwin LTD.

Banks, J. A. (1983). Multicultural education at the crossroads. *Phi Delta Kappan, 68*(8), 59.

Banks, J. A. (1984). *Teaching strategies for ethnic studies* (3rd ed.). Boston, MA: Allyn and Bacon, Inc.

Baptiste, H. P., Jr. (1979), *Multicultural education: A synopsis,* Washington, DC: University Press of America

Bogen, J. E. (1973). The other side of the brain: An appositional mind. In Robert E. Ornstein (Ed.), *The nature of human consciousness* (pp. 101-125). San Francisco, CA: W. H. Freeman & Co.

California State Board of Education. (1989). *Visual and performing arts framework for California public schools: Kindergarten through grade twelve.* Sacramento, CA: California Department of Education.

California State Board of Education. (1990). *Bilingual education handbook: Designing instruction for LEP students.*

Sacramento, CA: Bureau of Publications, Sales Unit..

Carter, L. C. (1984). The state of dance in education: Past and present. *Theory into Practice, 23*(4), 293-299.

Cecil, N. L., & Lauritzen, P. (1994). *Literacy and the arts for the integrated classroom: alternative ways of knowing.* White Plains, NY: Longman Publishing Group.

Chapman, J. M., (Ed). (1983). *Multicultural education: Suggested class activities.* Lansing, MI: Michigan State Board of Education.

Flinchbaugh, R. W. (1993). *The 21st century board of education.* Lancaster, PA: Technomic Publishing Company.

Francis, S. D. (1992). *A multicultural education project to promote the acceptance of culturally diverse students in the elementary schools.* Unpublished master's project. California State University, Pomona, California.

Galyean, B.C. (1981). The brain, intelligence and education: implications for Gifted programs. *A Journal on Gifted Education, 4*(1), 6-8.

Gardner, H. (1973). *The arts and human development.* New York: John Wiley & Sons.

Gardner, H. (1982). *Art, mind, and brain.* New York, NY: Basic Books.

Gardner, H. (1983). *Frames of mind.* New York, NY: Basic Books.

Gardner, H. (1990). *Art education and human development.* Los Angeles, CA: The J. Paul Getty Trust.

Geiger, C., & Rodriguez, D. M. (1993). *A social studies unit for the elementary school on the pilgrim experience.*

Unpublished master's project. California State University, Pomona, California.

Gezi, K. (1987). Issues in multicultural education. *Educational Research Quarterly, 6*(3), 5-13.

Gingrasso, S. H., & Stinson, S. (1989). Dance dynamics. *Journal of Physical Education, Recreation, and Dance, 60*(5), 31-60.

Guillermina, D. (1954). *Dances of México.* London: Max Parrish.

Hart, L. (1975). *How the brain works.* New York, NY: Basic Books.

Hawkins, A. (1964). *Creating through dance.* Englewood Cliffs, NJ: Prentice Hall.

History-Social Science Curriculum Framework and Criteria Committee. (1987). *History-Social science framework for California public school kindergarten through grade twelve.* Sacramento, CA: CDE Press, Sales Office.

Hollins, E. R. (1982). Beyond multicultural education. *Negro Educational Review, 33,* 140-145.

Howe, D. S. (1989, May/June). At the crossroads: The national dance association in the 1990's. *Arts in Education,* 44-47.

Kniep, W. M. (1989, October). Social studies within a global education. *Social Education,* 399-403.

Lockhart, A. (1966). *Modern dance: Building and teaching lessons.* Dubuque, IA: WM. C. Brown Company Publishers.

Logan, M. (1984). Dance in the schools: A personal account. *Theory Into Practice, 23*(4), 300-302.

Marich, A. (1991, February). Multimodels for multicultural dance. *Journal of Physical Education, Recreation and Dance,* 4-5

National Council for the Social Studies Task Force on Scope and Sequence. (1989, October). In search of a scope and sequence for social studies. *Social Education,* 376-385.

Olneck, M. R. (1990). The recurring dream: Symbolism and ideology in intercultural and multicultural education. *American Journal of Education, 98*(2), 147-174.

Overby, L. Y. (1992). Status of dance in education. *Eric Digest, 91*(5), 1-4.

Piaget, J. (1985). *Equilibration of cognitive structures.* Chicago, IL: University of Chicago Press.

Posey, E. (1988). Discipline-based arts education—developing a dance curriculum. *Journal of Physical Education, Recreation and Dance, 59*(9), 61-64

Ramirez, III, M., & Price-Williams, D. R. (1974). Cognitive styles of children of three ethnic groups in the United States. *Journal of Cross-*

Cultural Psychology, 5, 212-219

Ramirez, O. N. (1989). Social and political dimensions of folklorico dance: The binational dialectic of residual and emergent culture. *Western Folklore, 48,* 15-32.

Rosengren, F. H., Wiley, M. C., & Wiley, D. S. (1983). *Internationalizing your school: A handbook and resource guide for teachers, administrators, parents, and school board members.* New York: National Council of Foreign Language and International Studies.

Sagan, C. (1977). *The dragons of Eden.* New York, NY: Ballantine.

Saxe, D. W. (1989, September/October). Mary Sheldon Barnes and the introduction of social sciences in public schools. *The Social Studies,* 199-202.

Schwartz, P. (1991). Multicultural dance education in today's curriculum. *Journal of Physical Education, Recreation and Dance, 62*(2), 45-48

Sparshott, F. (1990). Contexts of dance. *Journal of Aesthetic Education, 24*(1), 73-87.

Stinson, S. (1989). Creative dance for preschool children. *Early Child Development and Care, 47,* 205-209.

Toor, F. (1947). *A treasury of Mexican folkways.* New York: Crown Publishers.

Trujillo, L.A. (1979). *History and significance of the Hispanic dance expression.* Washington, DC: U.S. Department of Education National Institute of Education Educational Resources Information Center.

Vygotsky, L. S. (1978). *Mind in society.* Cambridge, MA: Harvard University Press.

Weaver, V.P. (1988). Education that is multicultural and global: An imperative for economic and political survival. *Social Studies, 79*(3), 107-109

PART 2

CHAPTER 5

HISTORY OF MÉXICO'S FOLK MUSIC AND DANCES

México has a tremendous wealth of folk music and dances. Many of them an ancient heritage. Folk music exists everywhere in México. The spirit of the dance lives and palpitates in each one of the popular expressions of its people. It reflects the customs of long ago in the magnificent spectacles which speak of sentiments and longings of the great past. The dance in México presents such rich variety in modes and styles that it can be represented as a mosaic, seen as a panorama but one which generally conforms to conventional geographic divisions (Riveroll, 1947). The dances are classified under two headings, danzas and bailes. Danzas refer to dances of ceremonial character; bailes to those of a social nature. Both are translated "dance" in English.

Following the conquest, the Spaniards employed native musicians because they did not have any of their own. But later ignored them because they did not need them. Today folk music and musicians are greatly appreciated more than ever. There is true interest and enthusiasm in discovering the native dance, investigating it and learning it. This movement in favor of the danza and popular baile has a positive significance inasmuch as it constitutes a solid foundation for the advent of the Mexican Ballet. Within time, the ballet will be able to carry the richness of color, rhythm, and social content which animates it to the highest expression of culture in America (Riveroll, 1947).

Prior to the conquest, only men and boys played musical instruments, but the boys and girls learned to sing and dance together throughout their lives. Only boys received musical instruction after the Conquest in the first Catholic schools. The most famous being the one established by Fray Pedro de Gante at Texcoco in 1527 (Toor, 1947). Many natives became good musicians and were also skillful in making copies of the European instruments. Within a short period of time there were a sufficient number of skilled musicians for the numerous churches established. However, this form of musical education and training conflicted with the main interests of the Spanish conquerors. They felt that the natives were becoming too educated and spending too much time in schools. Consequentially, the indigenous people were not permitted to attend the schools and educate themselves. Thus, the schools were closed and the work of the missionaries came to an abrupt end (Toor, 1947).

Nevertheless, the musical education of the people continued, but not on the religious theme. The merchants found that they could sell more liquor by teaching the people to sing and play guitars. With the leniency of the laws and the opportunistic merchants, México was flooded with intoxicating drinks.

As time went on women sang less because they were unhappy with their social status. Except for the Seri and Huichol women and girls, singing was done in church. One would seldom hear a woman singing at her work. The people sang less after the Conquest because only those who are free and happy sing (Toor, 1947).

Since the 1910-20 Revolution conditions have changed. The people feel freer and are encouraged to sing. They need no longer fear to raise their voices or to sing their songs. Folk music is now popular everywhere. People sing and dance more than ever before and express the entire gamut of their emotions through their music.

The dances selected for this project were selected according to availability. All the dances for secular folk dances are in the form of song, called sones, jarabes and huapangos, the latter having a very marked rhythm. The tunes are light and gay; the verses picaresque and tender.

There are secular dances everywhere, but not danced to the same extent by all the people. Among the very primitive groups, women and girls do not dance them, even though some may take part in ritual dances.

The basis of practically all folk dances is the jarabes or sonas, names by which both the dances and tunes are designated, most of them being songs. Jarabe means a syrup or sweet drink in Spanish, but various dances introduced by the Spaniards in the form of zapateados were called jarbes (Toor, 1947). The literal meaning of son is "an agreeable sound." The dance songs began being called sones about the middle of the eighteenth century.

The Jarabe is among the oldest of Mexican dances. It is generally conceded that the Jarabe originated in the state of Jalisco and has been called the Jarabe Tapítio, the name applied to anything and everything coming from Jalisco (Tibbels, 1933). The Jarabe Tapítio is the Mexican national folk dance. The dance is internationally known and termed the official Jarabe. It is extensively used on Independence Day.

The jarabe consists of nine gay, captivating melodies and dance figures, the dancers meeting and moving around each other but always some distance apart. They dance with heel and toe, beating a strong rhythm to the music. The entire dance takes about ten minutes. At the end of the dance comes, “The Dove;” the man follows his partner as she dances around the broad brim of his sombrero. As the woman stoops to pick it up, he passes his right leg over her. The dancers finish by facing the audience, dancing back and forth, with the man’s arm around the girl. The girls wear the China Poblana costume and the men that of the charro. The Jarabe Tapatío is danced in many theaters, cabarets, secular fiestas, and rodeos. It awakens a joyous response with handclapping The dance is irresistibly gay and driving.

If this jarabe is danced by rancheros, it is even gayer and more fiery. The music is furnished by mariachis and singers. The dance may last for many hours with the dancers improvising verses and steps. The folk jarabes and sones are much simpler and are danced differently. The partners never touch each other. The woman dances slowly, modestly, and never looks at her partner. The man dances faster and holds himself stiff above the waist. The dancers are light and graceful. The men show their muscle control by dancing with a glass of water on top of their heads without dropping a drop, or tie or untie a knot in a sash or kerchief with their feet (Toor, 1947). There are no special costumes worn in these dances.

There are many formalized folk jarabes. El Jarabe de la Botella is very popular in Jalisco. It is very humorous and requires great dancing skills. The partners dance for a short time; then both take a drink from the same bottle of tequila, stand it on the floor and take turns dancing over it. As they dance a musician sings that they are not to spill the content. If the content is spilled it is replaced by a full bottle.

Sometimes jarabes are danced at funerals of young children and at weddings, and assume a ceremonial characteristic. In Chicomcuac many weddings begin with a jarabe. The parents of the bride dance with plates of food in their hands, others with jars of pulque on their heads, one person with a basket of tortillas and another with a live turkey. In Oasaca weddings, the jarabes and sones are called fandangos (Toor, 1947).

The Huapango is very widespread and popular in México. It is danced in all of the Huastecas, from the State of Tamaulipas to Vera Cruz. The Huapango is the dance of the platform. The dance is performed on a platform and is rhythmic in nature. Men and women face each other in files. The steps are simple, heel and toe, beating once with the heel and twice with the toe, but at times the men will introduce complex zapateados. The music consists of a series of sones, called huapangos. The music is played on violins, guitars and jaranas, the latter like a ukulele. In some areas harps are added. The musical rhythm is characterized by bringing down the fist or open hand on the strings of the guitars for the last note of each measure (Toor, 1947). With the beat of the feet, this dance is very gay and lively. Though the music and steps may be attributed to Europeans, this dance may be more related to the pre-Spanish mitotes, also performed on a platform. The word huapangos is derived from the Aztec word "cuah-panco-cuaitl," cuah meaning wood or log; ipan meaning on or over and co meaning place.

At one time huapangos were only danced by the higher social classes, but now many individuals take part in this dance. In many places, the haupangos constitute the weekly Saturday night dances. The dance goes on endlessly, but the musicians change the tunes and the singers improvise new verses. Many of these verses are humorous verses about mothers-in-law or some of an outstanding spectator.

Certain sones or huapangos are played for definite purposes, El Caiman and La Bamba, when a dancer is balancing a bottle or such feats are about to take place, they are announced and all the other dancers step to one side to watch and applaud (Toor, 1947). “El Torito” is a sign for the men to take out their handkerchiefs to play at bull fighting with their partners. “Los Panaderos” is played as a hint that the musicians want to rest, as well as a suggestion to the men to invite the girls for refreshments. Some huapangos go on for days, but they are never dull.

Michoacan has many other interesting dances besides the negritos. Los Viejitos, the little old men, is usually danced by younger individuals. The dancers begin by acting like decrepit old men. They do a series of virile zapateados to joyful sones played on a tiny stringed instrument, the jarana. The viejitos of the villages around Lake Pátzcuaro wear white cotton suits, long flaring trousers, embroidered at the bottom, a tunic with a red sash tied at the side and strong shoes (Toor, 1947). Their wide brimmed, low crowned hats are colored with ribbons crossed from the point and falling over the brim. A silk kerchief hangs around their necks and a white jorongo with colored stripes. The masks of these dancers are of light wood, carved and painted with old faces. Some of the masks are sad while others are smiling, with fibre air and some with beards. Each dancer carries a staff with an animal's head carved at the handle.

The musicians direct the dancers who try to outdo each other in steps and clowning. Los Viejitos is danced on secular occasions but mostly during religious fiestas.

The folk dance of Yucatán is the jarana. The dance, music and the function derive their name from the ukulele-like instrument, called the jarana. The word means noisy diversion. The steps for this dance consist of zapateados and the music of sones without words, played on jaranas, brass instruments and drums. The Cuban göiros or gourds may also be added.

Couples dance facing one another, the man with his hands behind his back and the girl raising her skirts slightly. At certain intervals, they pass one another and snap their fingers in a Spanish fashion. When the Torito is played, the couples play at bull fighting. During the dance, the musicians may frequently stop playing and someone shouts, “bomba,” a signal for the man to say a compliment to his partner (Toor, 1947). A dancer may compliment his partner by placing his hat on her head.

The village jaranas are different from the city communities. The dances serve as a ritual as well as a social function. Many are danced during novenas, offerings to saints, and at religious fiestas. These dances serve as opportunities for boys to meet girls.

During the annual religious fiesta in Chan Kom and other villages of the region, the jaranas are associated with the bullfights. The young men who dance them are called vaqueros. The girls are call vaqueros, the female counterpart. The dance may be called a vaqueria instead of a jarana. These dances always end with the Torito, in which the girl bullfighter tries to make the bull dancing opposite her lose his balance or step off the platform.

Canacuas, which means crowns in Tarascan, is a folk dance of the city, and surrounding villages of Uruapan, Michoacán. This dance is pre-Conquest in origin, and is associated with weddings. Youths and maidens assemble, the former carrying flowers on their heads, while the latter carries beautiful bouquets. The dancers offer the newly married couple useful objects for the new family and then dance together. This fiesta was called canacuas and still exists in various towns of Michoacan (Toor, 1947).

Many present day canacuas have similarities to the original canacuas. However, only young unmarried girls take part in them. During the dance, a young man, el indito, joins the girls to talk and dance a jarabe with one of them.

The present canacuas are still performed at weddings and other secular fiestas. They are also used to honor important guests in the community. The girls wear costumes after the Tarascan women and are called güaris. The costume consists of a pleated skirt, embroidered shirt, rebozo crossed in front, aprons, strings of colorful beads, and bright ribbons in the hair. Each girl carries a colorfully painted gourd bowl, called xicapexli. The gourd bowls are filled with flowers, fruit, and lacquered and clay toys.

A small orchestra of stringed instruments, including a harp, accompanies the dancers. The honored guest sits at a small table at the head of the two files that the dancers form. The audience sits in the patio or garden. The songs are very melodious and sentimental, with mixture of Spanish and Tarascan words.

The sones of Vera Cruz are very happy and gay. Couples dance with touching, to the music of a harp, violin, and guitar. There are two male singers who never take their hats off. The girls wear long cotton skirts with ruffles, a blouse, and a kerchief around the shoulders and crossed in front. Bows of colored ribbons adorn their hair. The men wear white cotton suits, with some color in the form of a sash or red silk kerchief (Toor, 1947). The partners dance quick zapateados. La Bamba is a famous sone from this region.

There are many other regional folk dances, like La Chilena from the coast of Guerrero and Oaxaca.

This dance is accompanied by sones. A mixed chorus may sing the song as an accompaniment to this dance. The girl is dressed in a black cotton skirt, ankle-length, with a two inch white strip around it near the bottom. The blouse is loose and big. She wears a red ribbon n her head and carries a big red bandanna. The boy wears a suite of unbleached muslin, red sash with the ends tucked in, shirttails tied in front and juaraches. He also carries a red bandanna (Johnston, 1935).

It would be impossible to describe all the ritual and secular dances. No one has listed all known dances and they are different in every region of México. Their varieties are as numerous as the places in which they are danced. However, all the dances, in general, express the vast emotional gamut of the Mexican people's diversified culture.

A Multi-unicultural Inclusion Mexican Regional Dances For Performing Arts

CHAPTER 6

SELECTED MÉXICAN REGIONAL DANCES

Los Viejitos (The Little Old Men)

Of all the typical danzas in the state of Michoacán, Los Viejitos is one of the best liked, and one which characterizes the comic feeling and the rhythmic precisions of the Tarascan Indians. During the religious festivities in most Michoacán villages, the dancers with mask-covered faces are always present. They lean wearily on their canes and appear to feel a senility which is very contradictory to the vigor of their young, strong bodies.

It is in the region which centers around Lake Pátzcuaro where the dance is performed. The dance group is almost always made of 12 members. The director of these is the Viejito who plays a small jarana, a stringed instrument used to accompany the whole dance. Each village variation imposed in the choreography and the general presentation of the group of dancers depend upon the artistic refinement of the dance director.

The dancer presents himself to the public in gay attire. On his head he wears a palm sombrero with a low round crown and a broad brim, trimmed with colored ribbons and paper flowers. He covers his face with a mask, which is either made of clay in the town of Santa Fé de l Laguna or made of wood from the tree named colorín. The grotesque form of the mask characterizes the Viejito as the eternal jester. The mask has traits of the Conquistadores. To give impression of his great age, the dancer covers his hear completely with a white cloth, and maguey fibers are attached to the edge of the mask to suggest a wig. He wears a colored undershirt and, around the neck, a large red silk'derchief. White calzones cut wide and full are used, the legs being embroidered at the bottom edge with a wide band of cross-stitch. Around the waist a long, narrow, colored woven sash, called ceñidor, is tied at the side and, often, hanging from it are tiny hand-woven bags. The dancer carries in his right hand the celebrated cane, roughly carved with the handle traditionally representing the head of an animal. Nowadays, it still looks like the head of some strange creature but is given this shape by the proper trimming of the roots of the bamboo from which the shaft of the cane is made. A small red or gray jorongo with long fringes is frequently worn. Stout black or brown shoes, cut all in one piece, with a strong heel, are common. The costume has been preserved in its entirety up to the present.

The music for this dance is very original, sweet, and delicate. A son for each step and figure gives a special effect when it is played on the jarana, the only musical instrument which is used (Fig. 5).[1]*

---

[1] Riveroll, Roberto. (1947). Mexican Dances. Riveroll's *Art Gallery.* Mexico.

El Jarabe Tapatio

El Jarabe Tapatio is the popular dance that is most characteristic of Mexico. It is generally danced by the residents of the state of Jalisco.

According to documented investigations by musicians, the Colonial epoch gave birth to the Jarabe. El Jarabe Tapatio has been converted into the National Dance of Mexico. The transplanting of the Spanish zapateado dances, principally the seguidilla, the fandango, the zambra and others, in time, gave origin to the choreographic expression which is known to have greatest Mexican flavor. The colonists danced these Spanish dances with a certain fidelity to the original execution; but little by little, the form of dancing them was modified. These were due to the influences of the local environment and the manner of feelings and interpreting the music of the criollos and mestizos. The Jarabe Tapatio had its origin in the Jarabe Gitano, which was common in Spain around the fifteenth century. In Mexico, the dance was influenced by the characteristic traits of the mestizo.

The costumes used by the dancers are worn by the Chino Poblana and the Charro. The Charro is a romantic figure. He wears long, tightly fitted trousers made of wool material or chamois leather, the full length of the outside of the leg being decorated with silver buttons which often represent horses' heads or horseshoes and are connected by a little chain. A less showy outfit may be trimmed with colored or white braid. He has a faja or sash of colored silk about his waist. Besides he usually wears a wide leather belt, embroidered with heavy silver or golden thread, which holds the pistol and cartridges. His short jacket is also of wool or chamois with braided decorations embroidered on the back, shoulders, and lapels. Underneath is a close fitting vest. A silk necktie is loosely tied in a bow at the neck of the white shirt. He wears pointed shoes, cut all in one piece, and he always has a wide-brimmed sombrero, the crown and the edge of the rim being embroidered with silver or gold thread. The sarape is flung over one shoulder. Also used is the guayabera, a garment which takes the place of a vest and jacket. It is a kind of blouse made of light material which allows great freedom of movement, trimmed with embroidery.

The costume for the girl, called China Poblana, is composed of white blouse, red skirt with sequins, white petticoat, rebozo, and high heeled shoes. The true origin can be found in the garments of Arabic origin used by the Chinas, a privileged group of distinguished ladies in the Colonial Period. The blouse is of white muslin or linen, having a rather low cut, square neck and short, tight sleeves. It is embroidered with brightly colored silk thread of tiny glass beads around the neck and on two or three narrow panels pendant from the front of the neck (Fig. 9). The gathered skirt is ankle length, made of red cotton flannel with a black design stamped on it. The skirt is called zagalejo, the material is known as castor. The black design is of the skirt is covered with varicolored sequins and the hem is edged with a two-or three-inch band of bright green satin. The same material is set on the top of the skirt in points. A rebozo of bright colored silk is worn around the waist, crossed over the back, one end brought forward over each shoulder and is tucked under itself at the waist. The ends hang out below.

A white petticoat with a starched, laced ruffle is used beneath the red skirt. Bright red or green, high-heeled shoes of satin are favored. Large pendant earrings, bracelets, and strings of shiny glass beads complete the attire of the Chino who adorns her braids with ribbons.[2]*

[2] Riveroll, Roberts. (1947). Mexican Dances. *Riveroll's Art Gallery*, Mexico.

El Jarabe de la Botella

The Jarabe de la Botella is characteristic of the states of Jalisco and Nayarit. Though danced principally on the coast, it is generally found in all the villages where they organize traditional fandangos, as the country fiestas are called.

Today the Jarabe de la Botella is danced in the form of a simple son. That is to say, the couple interprets the melodic theme which gives life and precision to their zapateado. They dance around and over the bottle of tequila, making a show of their ability to do it without touching the bottle. If one does upset it he or she is punished by having to pay the cost of what was spilled, all of which contributes to the gaiety of the fiesta.

Accompanying this dance is the group known as Mariachi, a group of players of sones. The musicians plan and sing in such a way that they impart great excitement and a contagious gaiety to the occasion warning the dancers not to throw the bottle by singing the following:

Andele compadre
Come on, compadre
Baile
Dance the bottle
Que se me la tira
If you throw it over
Me la vuelve llena.
You will return it
filled.
Andele compadre
Come on, compadre
Sigala bailando,
Keep on dancing,

Que se me la tira
If you throw it over
Me la va llenando.
You will refill it.

The Mariachi is usually composed of players of violins, guitar, vihuelas, a guitarrón, and a harp, all of which are stringed instruments, and are sometimes supplemented by trumpet, trombone, and clarinet. There are two versions of the origin of the name Mariachi. The best documented one assures us that it comes from a village in the state of Colima by this name, which is a Cora word; the Coras being an ethnic group which lives in that state. The other theory regards the word Mariachi as a derivation of the "marriage," ascribing it to the period of French Intervention in Mexico. This word was used to refer to the musicians who played at French weddings.

The dancers use the farmers' clothes typical of the region. The woman wears a wide percale skirt, which she lifts just enough for her stiffly starched white petticoat to be seen as she dances. Her blouse has long sleeves and, of course, she wears a rebozo de bolita. As ornaments she uses strings of beads around her neck and colored ribbons in her braids. She prefers high laced shoes. The man wears bleached cotton calzones, a red faja around the waist, a brightly colored shirt and, over this a white guayabera with its typical knot. He wears brown shoes, cut all in one piece, or heavy huaraches and around his neck he uses a gaily colored silk handkerchief. A low crowned hat of palm straw, so usual in the Bajio, and the inseparable wool sarape, enlivened by red designs, completes his outfit.[3]*

---

[3] Riveroll, Roberts. (1947). Mexican Dances. *Riveroll's Art Gallery*, Mexico.

La Zandunga

La Zandunga is the typical dance which is representative of the Isthmus of Tehuantepec. It is claimed that the Zandunga is of Chapeneco origin. The music is similar to the popular Spanish tune, La Petenera. In the Isthmus region, it is at Las Velas, the pagan festivals held in honor of the patron saint of a town or barrio, that the Zandunga and other sones are danced. Each barrio attempts to outdo the other in the organization and splendor of its Vela.

For these Velas, the women dress in their finest garments and their choicest jewels of gold and pearls. The skirt is called an olán. The olán is made of fine materials and embellished with rich embroidery. The complete costume is made up of a huipil chico, an enagua de olán, and a huipil grande. The huipil chico is a kind of quadrangular, loose fitting blouse, cut with a round neck and made of velvet or satin of a single bright color; it is embroidered with multicolored flowers which are delicately intertwined and similar in appearance to the work on Manila shawls. The second garment is called and enagua de olán, or ruffled skirt. The upper part of it is bright colored silk or velvet and the lower part is a ruffle, about 4 or 5 yards long and 12 to 15 inches wide, pleated with knife pleats stiffly starched and carefully ironed. It may be of sheet white cotton or of cotton lace. The same rich silk embroidered which decorates the huipil also adorns the skirt. Also, a special garment called a huipil grande is used. This resembles a baby's dress trimmed with a wide, stiffly starched white cotton lace ruffle at the sleeves and the hem line; a narrower ruffle edges the neck; the dress itself is usually made of colored cotton lace. The Tehuana uses this as headgear and the way in which it is worn shows whether the wearer is taking part in a religious ceremony or a pagan festival. The huipil grande is never used when dancing. The particular form of this huipil gave origin to a legend to the effect that it is an adaptation made by the Tehuanas of a priest's surplice found once on the beach.

Usually the Tehuanas go barefoot. However, those belonging to a certain social class, wear shoes. Both arranged their hair in braids with interwoven colored silk ribbons and are crossed in back, brought around to the front and held together by the ends of the ribbons tied in a bow. The costume is adorned with waist-length necklaces of small gold pieces, gold strand chains, and pendants made of large gold pieces.

The man wears white trousers, a white shirt with a turned-down collar, which is usually worn with the tails out and either a palm straw hat or a felt one, molded in a shape characteristic of the Isthmus. While dancing the man, shod with leather sandals or shoes, removes his hat.

The music is played on a marimba, an instrument typical of Chiapas. The music is considered a son composed of two parts. The first, known as the descanso, is slow and calm, and the second, known as the zapateado, is rapid and exciting. The music in this version is an arrangement of four themes and retains the air and rhythm of this music or the Isthmus.[4]

[4] Riveroll, Roberts. (1947). Mexican Dances. *Riveroll's Art Gallery*, Mexico.

La Bamba

On the coast of the state of Veracruz, in the lake villages near Alvarado and on the shores of the Papaloapan River, the Jarochos, as the natives of Veracruz are called, have preserved with purity their vernacular interpretation of the dance. Their dance form is commonly known as the Huapango.

Huapango is also the name given the poplar fiestas held along the coast in the states of Tamaulipas and Veracruz as well as those held inland in the Huasteca, which lies within the geographical area surrounding the junction of the states of Tamaulipas, Veracruz, San Luis Potosí. and Hidalgo. At these fiestas, the musicians sing couplets which are almost always improvised and which end with a !Ay!, sung in falsetto. As they sing, they play a harp, little jaranas, and bandolones to accompany the clicking heels of the huapanguero who dances on a wooden platform to enhance the resonance of the steps. The term huapango is derived from the

Nahuatl word meaning “on a wooden platform.” The fandango is known as a huapango which is the special kind of dance or the melodic structure of the music, or generally, the fiesta itself.

The steps of the La Bamba are very spectacular. The dancers, using only their feet, tie a long sash into a bow of two or four loops, meanwhile performing dance figures without losing the rhythm of the music.

In the huapangos, the men invite a partner to dance. The

dancing goes on in an enramada or in the patio of the Municipal Houses where a wooden platform has been constructed. The dancers translate into steps the sones played by the musicians who are singing:

Para bailar la Bamba,
Para bailar la Bamba
se necesita
Una poca de gracia
Una poca de gracia y
otra cosita
Y arriba y arriba,

Arriba y arriba, y
arriba iré;
Yo no soy marinero,
Yo no soy mariner,
Por ti seré, por ti
seré, por ti seré.

(translated into English)

To dance the Bamba,
To dance the Bamba
one needs
A little grace, A little
grace and a little
something else!
And onward and
onward,

Onward and onward
and onward I will go;
I am not a sailor,
I am not a sailor,
For you I will be, for
you I will be, for you
I will be.

The attire of the Jarochos is very colorful. The girl is dressed in a full organdy skirt of circular cut with a small train. It is trimmed with two wide-laced ruffles with black ribbons run through the beading at the top edges of the ruffles. The white blouse made of sheer muslin has puff sleeves and the front is trimmed with embroidery in black and white (Fig. 2). She wears an apron of shiny, black material made in a graceful style and trimmed with flowers embroidered in colored thread. Over the blouse the Jarocha, wearing white or black high-heeled shoes, uses a bright colored 'kerchief of sheer silk or gauze which is held in place by an attractive pin. Her two braids are crossed in back and a large colored bow with white gardenias in the hair crowns the finery. The outfit is not complete without both the white ruffled petticoat, which is seen when the dancer lifts her skirt in the swirl of steps, and the indispensable fan, which she coquettishly uses at the opportune moment. The costume is often supplemented by a plain colored reboza which, when dancing, the Jarocha wears loose over the back rolling the ends around the arms near the wrists. The man wears white drill pants or dark wool ones, a white shirt and over it a guayabera, also white. A silk handkerchief is worn around the neck, a silk faja or sash around the waist. He uses a cool hat or palm straw and his brown laced shoes are always well shined.[5]*

[5] Riveroll, Roberts. (1947). Mexican Dances. *Riveroll's Art Gallery*, Mexico.

Las Chiapanecas

Las Chiapanecas is from the state of Chiapas. It is primarily danced in the southern most region of Mexico near the Guatemalan border. It has a Spanish flavor in dress and step.

For Chiapanecas, the girl wears a black net dress that expends down to her ankles. Ribbons go around the skirt area with 12" to 18" separating them. Beautiful flowers have been sewn between the ribbons. Underneath she wears a black satin slip that extends from her shoulders to her ankles. Her hair can be worn in braids that are interwoven with ribbons or in a bun. She dances barefoot.

Boy wears an unbleached cotton suit-shirt and trousers. Around his waist he sometimes ties a sash. His hat has a shallow crown and a wide brim. He ties either a white or a red handkerchief around his neck or under his hat. He dances barefoot also.[6]

[6] Segovia, Eloisa and Wesley, Cindy. (1975). Las Chiapanecas. *Folkloricos Regionales de Mexico.*

A Multi-unicultural Inclusion Mexican Regional Dances For Performing Arts

Jarabe Michoacano

The state of Michoacán abounds in beautiful expressions of sones, gustos, and jarabes of a Tarascan-mestizo character. The Jarabe Michoacano is the local expression of the spirit of merriment awakened during the middle of the 19th century. The jarabe rose to popularity in the country as a dance mode appropriate to and expressive of the nature of the Mexican nationality.

The Jarabe Michoacano is relatively new. In both its music

and choreography it competes with El Tlaxcalteca, El Pateño, El Jarocho, El Mixteco, and other jarabes. It is composed of different sones whose arrangements is such that the music forms a unified whole. All these combinations of sones are ordered in a manner which allows the man to besiege his partner and dance around her closely. There are six parts to this Jarabe, each of which is a typical son that is exciting and full of emotion. In the paseo, the couple changes places. The paseo is characteristic of the old jarabes and the gustos of this region.

In the fandangos, jolgorios or simple family gatherings, the jaraberos, regarded as professional dancers because of their agility and skill, attire themselves in the typical costume of the mestizo rancho of the region. The woman wears a comely blouse and a colored skirt made with a waist band, decks herself with a rebozo palomo and braids ribbons into her hair. The man uses the ordinary clothes, consisting of pants, shirt, and the palm sombrero with wide brim and low, flat crown.

The woman dancers wear the best clothes of the Guaris, which is characteristic of the indigenous Purépechas. They wear a blouse or huanengo embroidered in colored thread in cross-stitch, a skirt known as a rollo and a white cotton cloth in back named resplandor. The rollo is a long piece of dark blue, black, or red woolen material. It may be as much as 50 inches wide and 5, 6 or even 10 yards long. The top edge is folded inside so that the skirt will be ankle length. One end is wrapped around the hips of the wearer and all of the remaining material is folded into overlapping pleats about three inches wide. For easier manipulation, the pleating is done in front and, when finished, is shifted to the back, leaving the front of the skirt perfectly plan and smooth and the back a mass of pleats. The rollo is securely held in place by means of various long, narrow, hand-woven ceñicores or sashes which are wrapped around and around the waist. The resplandor is an undergarment of coarse cotton cloth, a kind of petticoat, arranged in the same way as the rollo, its chief difference being that the material is wider. The extra width is allowed to come out above the top of the rollo and the full pleated part ripples across the back like a graceful fan. There is often a cross-stitch design worked on the bottom edge of this undergarment. The guari wears a medium size white or colored apron also adorned with cross-stitch designs, and the typical rebozo of Michoacán. This rebozo is usually dark blue with white or light blue stripes and is embellished with long fringes made with varicolored silk thread. She has bright pink ribbons intertwined in her braids and frequently she is adorned with beautiful silver ear-rings with pendants and a necklace formed with alternated beads of silver and coral, ending with a silver cross. When dancing the Jarabe, they usually wear shoes or huaraches.

The men use the lower crowned sombrero of abajeño style, a shirt with both cuffs and front embroidered in cross-stitch, and calzones which are rather wide at the top. If they are plain at the bottom edge, they are folded over and tied closely around the ankle; if they are richly embroidered at the bottom edge, they are cut full and are allowed to hang freely. In both cases, the typical colored faja is worn around the waist. The jarabero is shod with huaraches or shoes cut all in one piece. Thrown over his shoulder, he wears a wool sarape, ending always in long fringes. The Jarabe Michoacano is usually accompanied by musicians who play violins, guitars, and guitarrones.[7]

---

[7] Riveroll, Roberto. (1947). Mexican Dances. *Riveroll's Art Gallery.* Mexico.

Jarana Yucateca

The peninsula of Yucatán is the rich and legendary country of the indigenous Maya. The Conquistadores introduced the lively rhythms of the seguidilla and the Spanish zapateo into Yucatán, seat of the Mayan civilization. The Jarana Yucateca is a regional dance which is the equal of the jarabe or Huapango. It has a definite and unmistakable regional stamp in its music, costume, and choreography, in all of which vibrates the Mestizo spirit. This spirit in Yucatan was born of the marriage of the Spanish hidalgo with the Maya maiden.

In Yucatán the social gatherings where the regional dances are performed are still called Vaquerias. In the Vaquerias, the women wear white garments which denote the social condition of the wearer. For everyday use the terno is always made of cotton material and is much simpler than the one made for fiesta wear. A fiesta outfit may be cotton or china silk. Three separate garments make up the terno. The outermost article is a long hipil reaching below the calf of the leg. It is embroidered with cross-stitch in a wide border around the low cut square neck. The cross-stitch is called xokbil-chuy in Maya and nowadays is almost always a floral design. On very fine hipiles this embroidery is sometimes done on a separate square collar which is edged with narrow silk lace. For a fiesta hipil a six or eight-inch band of embroidery is placed just above the knees. Often silk insertion about two inches wide is used above the embroidery. Below the latter is an eight or nine inch flounce of silk lace. The second garment is the sayuela, worn under the hipil, and is an ankle length skirt gathered on a waistband. For a terno de jujo there is a wide border of cross-stitch just below her knees. The colorful designs show through the lace flounce of the hipil. Another similar flounce finishes the bottom edge of the sayuela. A fustan, which is simply a white petticoat trimmed with a white "store" embroidery ruffle, is worn under the sayuela. A silk rebozo is also used. It may be a rebozo de bolita or a plain one. At present ordinary high-heeled shoes are worn, but a generation ago a very special style was popular. The shoes were made of bright colored fabrics, especially satin, and embroidered in cross-stitch. The heels were high and the pointed toes turned up like shoes from the "Arabian Night". The mestiza arranges her long, shiny black hair at the back of her head in either a single knot, known as x'tuch in Maya, or a loop to each side of the center of the back. In either case, she pins a bright silk bow to the knot of the hair. A gold necklace with a medal or coin on it may be worn, but the final adornments are earrings and an exquisite rosary. Both of the latter are of gold filigree and coral. The gold filigree work of Yucatán is among the finer in the Republic and it is shown off to better advantage when worn with the beautiful mestiza costume.

The man dresses in well-starched and well-ironed pants made of dril. His guayabera is a variety peculiar to Yucatán, both white and colored ones being popular. A guayabera is hip length and is finished at the bottom by a decorative band, of the same material as the guayabera, stitched to the edge. Long sleeves with either double or single cuffs are used. The front opening of the guayabera is closed either by ordinary buttons or by gold studs.

The collar is generally worn opened and, when dancing the Jarana, a silk handkerchief is worn around the neck. Alpargatas is the name given to the open sandals which are worn without stockings. Those in present days use are made of stripes of patent leather about an inch wide. The top layer of leather is cut out and gay colors are laid underneath. Not so many years ago alpargatas were made by interweaving quarter inch strips of leather which in turn were worked with small designs. In both styles, heels are about one inch high, slanting inward a little; the toe of the sole has an off center point and turns up. The dancer's hat, sometimes called guano is known as jipi in Mérida. It is made in Bécal, Campeche and rivals the famous Panama hats of Ecuador.

The musical instruments played to accompany this dance are usually a guitar, violin, clarinet, trumpet, trombone, kettle drums, and a güiro. The güiro is a gourd, 12 to 15 inches long, with ridges cut into one side. A stick is scraped over the ridges to produce the desired sound effect. The Yucatecans give it the name of rascabuche. Rascar means to rasp or scrape; buche means crop (of a bird). The Jarana music is more influenced in its style and structure by Spanish music than any other Mexican folk music. It is played in tow rhythms, 3/4 and 6/8. The former is similar to the jota since it is written in 3/4 time and has a great similarity in its melodic structure. The 6/8 has all the characteristics so typical of the Spanish zapateado and, like this, is written in 6/8 time.

The production of the jaranas is abundant and enthusiastic since the Yucatecan composers are vey inspired and fight for the popularity of their work. Among the general public, jaranas are so popular that many pieces are rewritten in jarana rhythm.[8]*

[8] Riveroll, Roberto. (1947). Mexican Dances. *Riveroll's Art Gallery.* Mexico.

REFERENCES

Brewster, M. S. (1937). *Mexican and New Mexican folk dances.* Albuquerque, NM: University of New Mexico Press.

Campos, R. M. (1929). *El folklore literario de Mexico*. México, D.F.: Secretaria de Educación Pública.

Dickens, G. (1954). *Dances of Mexico.* London: Max Parrish.

Johnston, E. (1935). *Regional dances of Mexico.* Dallas, TX: B. Upshaw and Co.

Reuter, J. (1988). *La música popular de México.* México, D. F.: Panorama Editorial, S. S.

Riveroll, R. (1947). Mexican Dances. *Riveroll's Art Gallery*, México.

Ruiz, B. *Breve historia de la danza en Mexico.* México, D. F.: Biblioteca Minima Mexicana.

Schwendener, N., & Schwendener, T. (1934). *Legends and dances of old México.* New York. NY: A. S. Barnes and Company.

Segovia, E. M., & Wesley, C. C. (1975). *Folklóricos regionales de México.* Colton: C and E Prensa.

Songs in Spanish for intermediate. (1991). New York, NY: Macmillan Publishing Company.

Toor, F. (1947). A treasury of Mexican folkways. New York, NY: Crown Publishers, Inc.

DISCOGRAPHY

Bailables Escolares. Mariachi Los Toritos. AZ Discos AZ 011.

Bailables Escolares. Mariachi Los Toritos. AZ Discos AZ 036.

Bailes Regionales de Mexico. RCA MKL 1448.

Bailes Tipicos Mexicanos Vol. 1. Corito CI 121.

Bailes Tipicos Mexicanos. Discos Columbia MDC 1086.

Ballet Folklorico de Mexico. RCA MKS LF 18032.

Bonito Veracruz. Conjunto Jarocho Villa del Mar de Angel Valencia Cuate's CU 534.

Cantos y Danzas de Mexico. Ballet Aztlán Musart ED 875.

Danzas y Jarabes. Mariachi Monumental de Silvestre Vargas Discos Columbia MDC 1086

Danzas Mexicanas. Columbia DCA 149.

El Mejor Mariachi del Mundo. RCA MKS 1224 Argano DKL 1-3036

Fandango Jarocho. Jacinto Gatica-su Arpa y su Conjunto Cuate's CU 534

Fantasia Mexicana. Chucho Zarzosa y su Orquesta RCA CFS 446(e).

Fiesta Mexicana. Capitol T 10181.

Folklore de la Campina Mexicana. Peerless APM-19.

Fiesta del Sol Jalisciense. El Mariachi Mexico en Accion Antilla 631.

La Cacahuata. Los Broncos de Reynosa ECO 347.

La Zandunga. Marimba Oro y Plata de Arturo Cordero Cuate's CU507.

Las Olas-Sones Jaliscienses. Memo Quintero Mariachi Los Michoacanos

Azteca AM 8009

Las Mañanitas. Mariachi Mexico de Pepe Villa Discos FM-144.

Mariachi Jalisco de Pepe Villa. CBS EPC 340 (45 RPM).

Mariachi-Soul of Mexico. Epic Mono LF 18032.

Polka. Tony de la Rosa Ideal 45-2230-A.

Sones Jaliscienses. Caytronics CYS 1196.

Sones Jaliscienses. Mariachi Tepatitlán Tuna TU 8008

Sones Jarochos. Con los Nacioales de Jacinto Gatica.

Sones Jarochos. Conjunto Los Costeros Tuna TU 8007.

The Colorful Folkore of Mexico. Falcon FLP 2015.

Veracruz Hermoso. Conjunto Jarocho Medelin de Lino Chavez RCA Camden CAM-28.

GLOSSARY

Singular

Plural

Masculine El

Los

Feminine La

Las

Alpargatas–Leather sandals made and worn in Yucatan.

Arpero–Harp player.

Atole, El–The corn gruel. Name of a son played for jarabes.

Ay–An exclamatory sound.

Baile–A dance of social nature, predominantly mestizo and creole in origin.

Baoji–Lowlands.

Bamba, La–Name of a dance from Veracruz.

Bandolon–A stringed instrument of 6 strings belonging to the lute family. It is frequently used in the typical Mexican string ensemble to strengthen the tone produced by instruments of high pitched range.

Bomba–Shout used when dancing the Jarana as signal for the

man to say a compliment to his partner.

Bule–Gourd.

Cacao–Tree, the fruit of which is made into chocolate.

Calzones–White bleached cotton pants which look very much like pajamas. They are cut very full in the crotch which allows sufficient fullness for closing the front in a wrap-around fashion. A belt of the same material is stitched to the top edge. The long ends of the belt continue around the waist in the direction of the overlapped pieces and are tied to hold the calzones in place. The bottoms of the legs sometimes hang loosely, sometimes they are tapered and tied tightly around the ankle. In rainy weather they are often rolled to the knee to keep them clean and dry.

Carrerita–Dance step consisting of a series of small, quick steps.

Castor–Material for the China Poblana skirt.

Ceñidor–Long Sash.

Charro–Mexican cowboy. Male dancer in the Jarabe Tapatio.

Chiapaneco–Pertaining to Chiapas, the southernmost state of Mexico.

China Poblana–The female dancer in the Jarabe Tapatio.

Cojito, El–eh Little Cripple, name of a son played for jarabes.

Comadre–Woman related through god parenthood.

Compadre–Man related through godparenthood.

Conquistadores–Conqueroros The Spanish conquerors of the New World are often referred to a "Los Conquistadores."

Cruz, La–The Cross. Name of a step in Los Viejitos.

Danza–A dance of ceremonial character and usually of strong Pre-Columbian influence.

Danza de los Viejitos–Dance of the Little Old Men.

Descanso–Rest. In Mexican mestizo dances a descanso refers to a part of the music which is relatively slower and more calm than the rest of the piece.

Diana–Name of the music played as the last step of the Jarabe Tapatio. It is very gay and very popular. On other occasions it is often played with great speed to indicate a sign of approval.

Durazno, El–The Peach, name of a son played for jarabes.

Enagua de Olán–The Tehuana's shirt which has a wide ruffle at the bottom edge.

Enanos, Los–The Dwarfs, name of a son played for jarabes.

Enramada–An open air structure consisting of a roof supported by forked posts. Heavy poles are placed in the crotches of the posts and lashed together at the points of juncture. Over them are laid bamboo poles and leaves. They are piled thickly enough to make the space beneath shady and cool.

Espinado, El–The Thorny One, name of a son played for jarabes.

Faja–A long wide sash.

Fandango–Local name for a fiesta in the states of Jalisco, Nayarit and Veracruz. It is also the name of a Spanish dance.

Fiesta–A celebration, a festival. A fiesta may be large or small, simple or elaborate. A birthday party is a fiesta;

likewise a celebration honoring a patron saint and lasting 8 or 10 days is fiesta.

Finca–Ranch.

Fustán–White petticoat, part of the Yucatecan woman's costume.

Gala–A custom pertaining to Jarana dancing.

Guachapeo–A dance formerly done at Yucatán.

Guachapeadores–Dancers of the Guachapeo, the forerunner of the Jarana.

Guajito, El–The Little Squash, name of a son played for jarabes.

Guari–Women in Tarascan.

Güari–A gourd used as part of the musical accompaniment for the Jarana Yucateca.

Guitarrero–Guitar player.

Guitarrón–A very large guitar having five strings turned in fourths. It serves as a contrabass instrument for the group of players known as "Mariachi."

Gustos–A son or popular gathering.

Hidalgo–Spanish nobleman.

Hipil–The Yucatecan name for "huipil." The Yucatecan hipil is almost ankle length in contrast to the Tehuantepec huipil which is barely hip length.

Huanengo–Tarascan name for an unfitted garment which serves as a blouse. It is shaped very much like a pillowcase with a slit made for the head to pass through. It is embroidered around the neck and the arm openings. It is the same shape as the garment elsewhere known as huipil.

Huapango–The typical dance of the Huasteca region. It is also common along the coast of

Tamaulipas and Veracruz. It is also the local name for fiesta in the same region and the name of the music played for huapango dances.

Huapanguero–A Huapango dancer.

Huaraches–Woven leather shoes. They are made in many parts of the Republic, the style varying with the locality.

Huipil–An unfitted garment which serves as a waist. It is similar in shape to a pillow case with a vertical slit cut to serve as a neck. It is generally worn hanging loosely outside, and not tucked into the skirt.

Huipil chico–Small huipil worn by the Tehuanas.

Huipil grande–Large huipil, the headgear of the Tehuanas.

Jarabe–Literally, the word jarabe means "syrup" but used in relation to dances, it refers, to a mestizo dance os Spanish Colonial origin but truly Mexican in character.

Jarabe de la Botella, El–The Jarabe of the Bottle, a mestizo dance of the states of Jalisco and Nayarit.

Jarabe Michoacano, El.–The Michoacán Jarabe, a mestizo

dance of the state of Michoacán.

Jarabe Tapatío, El–Officially designated as the National Dance. It is a mestizo dance of Spanish Colonia origin. Tapatío, pertaining to the state of Jalisco.

Jaraberos–Jarabe dancers.

Jarana–A small stringed instrument. It is like a small sized guitar and has eight strings. Also the usual name for the Jarana Yucateca.

Jarana Yucateca, La–The local dance of Yucatán. It is also

danced in parts of Campeche and Quintana Roo.

Jaranita–diminutive of jarana.

Jarocha–County Woman of Veracruz.

Jarochita–Diminutive of Jarocha.

Jarocho, El–The Veracruz country man.

Jarro, El–The Jug, name of a son played for jarabes.

Jipi–Name commonly given in Mérida to a straw hat woven in Bécal, Campeche. More elegantly, it is referred to as "Jipijapa."

Jolgorio–Popular gathering.

Jorongo–A medium size sarape, worn with the head through the slit. The ends hang loosely in front and in back.

Jota–A Spanish dance from Aragón.

Maguey–Century plant that furnishes pulque and strong fibers.

Mariachi–A typical Mexican group of musicians.

Maya–A tightly fitted undershirt. It is factory made, knitted of cotton.

Mestizo–A person of mixed Spanish and Indian ancestry. Fem. Mestiza.

Mexteco, El–The Mixtecan, name of a jarabe.

Montejos–Spanish family which led the Conquest of Yucatán.

Nahuatl–Language spoken by the Aztec people.

Olán–ruffle.

Palomo, El–The Dove, name of a son played for both the Jarabe Tapatío and the Jarabe de la Botella.

Paseo, El–The promenade. In several of the regional

dances there is a paseo. It generally takes the form of walking step and gives the dancers a chance to rest without discontinuing their performance.

<u>Pasitos</u>–Small steps.

<u>Pasitos seguidos</u>–Small successive steps.

<u>Pespunteado</u>–Dance step using only the toe of the foot for vigorous stamping.

<u>Picado, El</u>–The Piqued one, name of a son and a step of La Bamba.

P'iris cab–Maya phrase meaning "the snapping of the fingers"

Pulque–Mexican typical drink made from the juice of maguey.

Purépecha–A Tarascan word which the Tarascan people used in referring to themselves. The Spaniards called them "Tarascans."

Quexquemetl-Mex.–A garment which slips over the head and is worn like a short cape. Rarely is it woven in one piece. Usually it is two rectangular pieces joined in such a way as to give the garment a triangular appearance in both front and back.

Raspador–Scraper, rash. It is a noise-making instrument.

Rebozo–A garment for women which combines the advantages of both a shawl and a scarf.

Rebozo de bolita–A Rebozo decorated with tiny white designs. Bolita refers to the designs which are similar to polka dots.

Rebozo palomo–Is one which has its wide fringe at each end decorated with silk threads in many colors.

Redoble–A dance step using rapid and continuous stamping with the heel.

Repiqueteo–A dance step consisting of a continuous swaying motion of the raised leg.

Respandor–White cotton cloth undergarment worn by the Tarascan women.

Rollo–Skirt worn by most Tarascan women.

Santa Cruz, La–The Holy Cross.

Sarape–The English word is "serape."

Sayuela–Garment worn by the Yucatecan mestiza.

Seguidilla–A popular Spanish tune and dance.

Se quieres, vámonos, te llevaré–"If you desire, let us go away, I shall carry you off," name of a son played for the Jarabe Tapatío.

Sombrero–Hat.

Son–A short musical composition which is usually made up of two parts having 16 measures each.

Taconeo, El–A dance step using only the heel of the foot for vigorous stamping. It is similar to the redouble in timing. Name of a son and step of La Bamba.

Tehuana–A woman of Tehuantepec.

Terno–Costume of Yucatecan mestiza.

Terno de lujo–Luxury costume of Yucatecan mestiza.

Velas, Las–Local name for fiestas in Tehuantepec, Oaxaca.

Vihuela–Vernacular form for guitar.

Xokbil-chuy–Maya word meaning "cross-stitch."

X'tuch–Maya name for a large knot of hair at the back of the head.

Zagalejo–Name given the red flannel skirt worn by the China Poblana.

Zandunga, La–The typical mestizo dance of Tehuantepec, Oaxaca.

Zapateado–A dance step in which the foot stamps the floor using the whole sole of the foot. It may be repeated as many times and in whatever rhythm the music and the fancy of the dancer dictate.

Zapateo–See zapateado.

ABOUT THE AUTHOR

Dr. Rodríguez is an educational leader focused on supporting local, state and national initiatives and programs. Dr. Rodriguez is a member of various educational organizations, including, the California League of High Schools and Association of California Administrators, as well as a California Awards for Performance Excellence California state senior examiner, Distinguished Schools, Schools to Watch and Gold Ribbon Awards.

Dr. Rodríguez has been in the educational profession for over

thirty-six years, having served as an elementary teacher, high school guidance counselor, and high school principal, in addition to, lecturer/presenter for state, national and higher education.

Contact and visit Dr. Paul A. Rodriguez at

par913@me.com

http://www.par913edu.com

http://www.californiacommoncorestandards.com

www.ingramcontent.com/pod-product-compliance
Lightning Source LLC
LaVergne TN
LVHW020708110826
845149LV00012B/2161

* 9 7 8 0 9 8 6 3 0 6 5 4 9 *